CHRIS HUMFREY'S
AWESOME AUSTRALIAN ANIMALS

To view the videos scan the QR codes with your phone or go to newhollandpublishers.com/awesomeaust and enter the unique codes

CHRIS HUMFREY'S
AWESOME AUSTRALIAN ANIMALS

CONTENTS

A WALK ON THE WILD SIDE ...

Welcome into my *wild* world of Australian wildlife. My earliest childhood memories are of being surrounded by animals. I have always marvelled at the extraordinary beauty of creatures, and the amazing jobs each and every species has in maintaining healthy ecosystems.

Luckily for me, I grew up with a very supportive mum and dad who helped nurture my wonderment for nature. When I was a kid, I had a veritable zoo in my very own back yard. From a young age, I was heavily involved in my local Field Naturalists group, allowing me access to fabulous wildlife experts and mentors. My thirst for learning led me to study a Bachelor of Science at the University of Melbourne, majoring in Zoology and Botany.

My home country of Australia is crammed full with totally awesome, unique and sometimes downright weird animals. I hope to share my fascination and knowledge of wildlife with you! If we love something, and understand it, we'll strive harder to save it.

Never before has our planet faced so many environmental challenges. Every animal species has a job to do, an ecological niche. We can't just save our favourites – we have to protect the scary, bizarre, 'not so attractive', and sometimes dangerous creatures too.

In a healthy world, all animals are interconnected and vital for balance. The protection of biodiversity also means a healthier and happier life for people too. Education and knowledge is definitely the key to conservation.

I hope that you spend many wonderful and engaging hours reading and re-reading my book. Enjoy my video clips too!

Are you ready to take a walk on the wild side?

Chris Humfrey
Zoologist

Shingleback

Tiliqua rugosa

'The lizard with many names.'

Thank goodness for universal binomial names – also known as Latin names – which name the species *Tiliqua rugosa* – this translates to 'blue-tongued lizard with wrinkly skin.' That certainly makes a lot of sense.

In Australia, there are five families of lizards which call the continent home. I'd love you to meet one of my all-time favourite lizards, the Shingleback.

What's in a name?

Some people know this animal as the bog-eye, stumpy-tail, bob-tail, two-headed lizard, or even the pine-cone lizard… the list goes on. In fact, it has more common names than any other lizard in Australia.

Classification

KINGDOM:	Animalia
PHYLUM:	Chordata
CLASS:	Reptilia
ORDER:	Squamata
FAMILY:	Scincidae
GENUS:	*Tiliqua*
SPECIES:	*rugosa*

Rubbish left by humans, such as sheet iron, refrigerators and car bodies will suit a Shingleback as a place to shelter. They even retreat into burrows dug by other animals.

Where is it found?

This large member of the skink family is widespread and found in most dry and arid regions across southern parts of Australia. Its large range is one of the reasons that this lizard has so many different names, which vary from location to location. Shinglebacks prefer open country with shrubs, leaf litter and plenty of rocks and timber to shelter beneath.

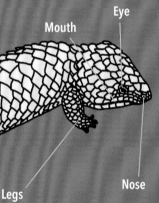

Eye
Mouth
Imbricate scales
Tail
Legs
Nose

They aren't particularly fussy about where they shelter.

Amazing morphology and adaptations

These thick-set lizards are ectothermic or cold-blooded, which means that they heat up their body by utilising their external environment. The large ossified (bony) scales are highly vascularised with blood vessels and are perfectly designed for warming their bodies in the sun – a process known as thermoregulation.

7

The scales are like built-in solar panels. That's much easier than the way we do it – we need to eat food to keep ourselves warm.

They don't need to go to the shops to buy new clothes – that's much cheaper than the way we do it.

The hard bony scales also offer protection from attack by would-be predators, such as raptors, goannas, foxes or even dingos.

As this lizard grows bigger it sheds its skin to reveal a shiny new one underneath. This process is also known ecdysis.

The Shingleback has perfect camouflage for a terrestrial (ground-dwelling) way of life.

It blends in perfectly to the dry environments which it inhabits, making it hard for hungry predators to detect it.

Shinglebacks have short stumpy legs and are not renowned for their speed.

If attacked, this lizard doesn't back down. It opens up its wide mouth and defiantly displays the bright blue tongue. Predators think twice about attacking a Shingleback. Although they have relatively small teeth, they make up for this with a powerful 'finger-crunching' bite. Their impressive jaw pressure assists them in cracking the exoskeletons of arthropods and snail shells.

They can't run very fast with those short little legs... Hey that's my problem too!

Their jaws are like Christmas nutcrackers – **OUCH**.

That's **soooo** confusing. Predators would think twice about eating a two-headed lizard. You could get your nose bitten off.

To trick predators, this ingenious lizard pretends it has two heads. Its fat bulbous tail turns around to face in the same direction as its head, and both pairs of feet face in the same direction as well.

Finally, if these defence mechanisms don't work, the Shingleback will release the contents of its bowels... and **pooooooo** all over you! **THAT IS DISGUSTING!**

Their chunky tail is filled with fat stores… a bit like a camel's hump. It enables the Shingleback to survive without food for a long period of time.

That certainly beats a school lunch box.

This amazing survival expert can survive without eating a meal for up to three months.

If that was me I think I'd have a grumbly tummy.

These prehistoric lizards have the ability to aestivate, where they become inactive for long periods of time, requiring very little energy input. **WOW!**

This amazing survival expert is an omnivore, and is definitely not a fussy eater. In fact the Shingleback is a real 'garbage-guts,' eating almost everything… fruit, flowers, vegetables, meat, even carrion (rotting flesh).

Hey, did you see him poke out his tongue? Don't worry, he's not being rude or cheeky… he's tasting the air and sensing his environment.

When you live in the arid lands of Australia you can't afford to be a 'picky' eater because you never know when your next meal will be available.

The Shingleback is a very important seed disperser of native plants. They have a large roaming territory, but they always seem to know where they are going.

They eat the flowers and 'poop' out the seeds, spreading them across Australia's barren landscape. That's their job, they are gardeners of the outback… that's their ecological niche.

Life cycle

Shinglebacks are solitary in nature, and generally live by themselves except during the breeding season. Each spring they search out a mate, and usually it's the same one each year, making this lizard a monogamous breeder.

That's because when baby Shinglebacks are born... the babies are HUGE.

Shinglebacks are viviparous, meaning that the female gives birth to live young. The gestation period is up to five months. They only give birth to one to three live babies, which are born as a smaller but exact replica of their parents.

These incredible arid survivors can live up to 50 years in the wild.

They mate for life.

Threats

Sadly, many Shinglebacks fall victim to vehicles on Australia's outback roads. Because of their 'sun-worshipping' behaviour, they seek out the warm surface of roads, and often get run over.

Wedge-tailed Eagles, Dingos, goannas and venomous snakes are among the Shingleback's natural predators. Introduced feral predators such as the European Red Fox, dogs and feral cats also see this enigmatic skink as easy prey for a quick snack.

Degradation of this lizard's habitat through farming practices and land clearance has contributed to noticeable population declines.

Male Shinglebacks generally have bigger 'boofier' heads than the females. Interestingly enough, females can grow longer and larger in size.

What can we do to help Shinglebacks out?

A wildlife license is needed to keep a Shingleback as a pet in Australia. It is illegal to take an animal from the wild – they are protected by law.

Keep your eyes open for lizards basking on country roads. Be responsible pet owners, walk your dog on a lead, and keep your pet cat indoors, day and night. You can also create suitable habitats where lizards can live.

SCAN HERE
to watch a WILD clip

azazer

Rough-throated Leaf-tailed Gecko

Saltuarius salebrosus

'One of Australia's largest gecko species, this cryptic denizen of Queensland's forests spends most of its life clinging to sandstone walls in caves or onto the sides of trees, perfectly camouflaged from predators and unsuspecting prey.'

What's in a name?

Their genus name **Saltuarius** means 'keeper of the forest,' and their species name *salebrosus* is Latin for 'rough.'

Classification

KINGDOM: Animalia
PHYLUM: Chordata
CLASS: Reptilia
ORDER: Squamata
FAMILY: Carphodactylidae
GENUS: *Saltuarius*
SPECIES: *salebrosus*

Where is it found?

There are many different species of leaf-tailed geckos in Australia, some are still being discovered and classified. This particular species is found in the ancient sandstone escarpment region of central tropical Queensland.

Amazing morphology and adaptations

The leaf-tailed gecko belongs to the class Reptilia. Reptiles are covered in scaly skin, and they do not sweat.

Clawed toes

Tubercles

Cartilaginous tail

Eyes

Long tongue

Caudal lure

Hey, they don't need to wear deodorant... that's **amazing**.

Australian geckos don't have eyelids, so they use their long flexible tongues to wash and clean their face.

They don't need to use a face-washer.

15

Are you nocturnal?...
Mum and dad might beg to differ with you... especially on a Saturday night.

This species is arboreal, meaning 'tree loving,' and has huge elliptical eyes which enable it to see exceptionally well at night. Animals which are mostly active at night-time are known as nocturnal. Humans are diurnal, which

This gecko's huge cartilaginous tail looks just like a flattened leaf – a perfect design for sitting still and blending in to its habitat. Adorned by a myriad of 'blotches and splotches' this cryptic gecko is a master of disguise, hiding from potential predators such as owls, frogmouths, goannas and tree snakes.

It's like a built-in school lunch box.

The fat-filled tail is an ingenious way to survive through tough times when food is scarce. The tail can sustain this lizard for many months without the need to eat.

If a predator grabs this gecko by the tail, they can quickly drop their tail as a decoy, and make a hasty escape, thus avoiding becoming a tasty snack. This is called **autotomy**. The tail is made of cartilage (not bone), and the gecko has the ability to regenerate its tail, albeit not as pretty or as detailed as the original one.

Leaf-tailed geckos have a caudal lure on the tip of their tail, which they wriggle to attract small insect prey. Once an insect is enticed, this ambush predator deftly pounces on its unsuspecting dinner.

Australian leaf-tailed geckos can change their colour depending on their body temperature needs. They are ectothermic, which means that they heat up their body using the external environment (source). They can change their overall body colour, making it darker to absorb more heat from the sun's rays, or when too hot they reflect the sun's energy by turning a paler shade. **WOW – that's incredible.**

A highly voracious predator, the Australian leaf-tailed gecko actively hunts for insects and other small arthropods. It doesn't need to drink water from a puddle or stream – instead water collects and pools on its 'prickly' scales, which it can readily lick off to drink. These bumpy scales are called tubercles.

YUK! WOW... no need for a drinking straw... that's sustainable living.

17

The gecko's rough skin feels like sandpaper – kind of like dad's face in the morning before he has a shave.

Unlike you and I, when this lizard grows larger, it sheds its skin like a dirty old sock.

Hey, that's much cheaper than the way we do it – by buying clothes at the shop.

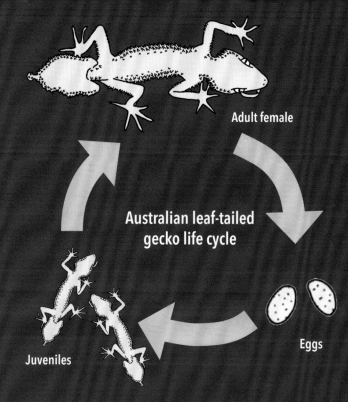

Australian leaf-tailed gecko life cycle

Adult female

Eggs

Juveniles

Life cycle

Australian leaf-tailed geckos are oviparous, which means that they lay eggs to reproduce. Usually laying two eggs, often producing many clutches over the breeding season, the baby geckos hatch out as mini replicas of the parents. Incubation can take up to 120 days – that's a long time for a small animal. But once hatched, a baby gecko doesn't receive any maternal care from its mum.

Australian leaf-tailed geckos have been known to live up to 20 years in captivity.

This particular species has sharp claws for gripping onto vertical surfaces as it climbs. Most people are familiar with Asian House Geckos, which have adhesive discs to climb up walls and glass.

When provoked, this lizard has been known to flay around its huge tail as a decoy, often hissing or wheezing to startle predators.

Threats

Although considered secure, this species of lizard has a range covering a relatively small area. Loss of habitat through land clearing, climate change, bush fires and introduced predators such as cats and foxes could threaten localised populations of this magnificent reptile.

SCAN HERE
to watch a WILD clip

exogof

Lace Monitor

Varanus varius

'Australia's second-largest lizard.'

This formidable monitor is an expert hunter, carnivorous in nature… it loves to eat meat. It is a very close cousin to the world's largest lizard… the Komodo Dragon.

What's in a name?

The genus name **Varanus** is derived from an Arabic name meaning 'dragon' or 'lizard beast.'

The species name **varius** relates to the high polymorphic variation in colour and pattern of this lizard in the wild.

Often called a goanna in Australia, early European settlers derived this name from the more familiar iguana lizard from the Americas.

Every Lace Monitor's pattern is different and unique – just like human fingerprints.

Classification

KINGDOM:	Animalia
PHYLUM:	Chordata
CLASS:	Reptilia
ORDER:	Squamata
FAMILY:	Varanidae
GENUS:	*Varanus*
SPECIES:	*varius*

Where is it found?

The Lace Monitor lives along the eastern side of Australia, occupying a diverse range of habitats and environments. It prefers to live in tall open woodlands from northern Queensland, all the way down the east coast of Australia, across northern Victoria to the south-eastern corner of South Australia. It is classified as an endangered species in the state of Victoria.

Amazing facts

Males grow larger than females, reaching just over 2 metres in length.

This species belongs to the monitor family – the only group of lizards in Australia with a forked or bifurcated tongue. It uses its two-pronged tongue to 'sniff' out potential prey.

That is so **COOL** – they can smell in stereo!

Armed with tough skin, razor-sharp teeth, long powerful claws, a tail like a 'bull-whip' and necrotic saliva in their mouth, this is definitely one Australian lizard which you don't want to mess with.

Sadly, in the southern parts of its range, this wonderful lizard is classified as endangered due to loss of habitat, road strike and introduced predators such as Red Foxes and feral cats which eat their young.

Humans have destroyed Lace Monitor habitat for collection of firewood and land clearing for development and farming purposes.

In the southern part of its range, this lizard is often jet black in colouration. The darker heat-absorbing scales enable it to warm up more quickly, meaning that it can survive in cooler, sometimes freezing environments. They also have the ability to flatten out their large bodies to increase their surface in order to heat up more quickly.

It's like having a built-in solar panel – that's amazing.

The skin feels like the security mesh on the front door of your house.

Their razor-sharp teeth are perfectly designed for grabbing, holding and tearing flesh off their prey – or from a would-be attacker.

This aptly named 'monitor' lizard is always on the lookout for food, constantly monitoring its environment for potential prey. The flexible forked tongue constantly flicks out of the mouth in the search for snakes, lizards, birds, bird eggs, arthropods and mammals. Lace Monitors are even happy to snack on rotting flesh – **YUK!**

Lace Monitors are covered in thick scales which can deflect the fangs of venomous snakes if attacked.

As Lace Monitors grow larger, they shed their skin. In scientific terms this is known as **ecdysis**. When they slough their old skin, they have a shiny new skin underneath.

The monitor is armed with a tail like a 'bull-whip,' which is a formidable weapon to use against attack from a potential predator such as a Dingo.

You'd think twice about eating a Lace Monitor if you were whacked on the nose.

The exceptionally long tail accounts for two-thirds of their body length.

Lace Monitor saliva is mildly venomous, [h...] necrotic properties which damage muscl[e...] cause profuse bleeding. A bite from this [...] is extremely painful, causing severe swel[ling...] infection, and requiring immediate medi[cal] attention.

This lizard's sense of smell is super. Its [...] bifurcated tongued is perfectly adapted [...] transferring scent molecules to the Jacob[son's] organ in the roof of the mouth. This ama[zing] sense organ helps the lizard to locate potential food, predators, competitors a[nd] mates, all from just flicking out its tongu[e.] **WOW**.

Their powerful limbs and dagger[ed] claws enable Lace Monitors to easily sca[le] even the tallest and straightest of trees.

They truly are **the ninjas** of the reptile world.

Life cycle

Lace Monitors are oviparous, which means that they lay eggs to reproduce. Females source termite mounds to deposit their eggs into. With their sharp claws, they excavate an egg chamber, depositing usually up to 12 eggs. The female fills in the opening of the hole and seals the eggs in. Then incubation can take up to seven months, with the heat of the termite colony helping the lizard's eggs to incubate over the winter period, hatching in the warmer months of the Australian spring/summer. Once the monitor hatchlings emerge from their eggs, the female returns to free them... by digging them out.

Wow, that's one great MUM.

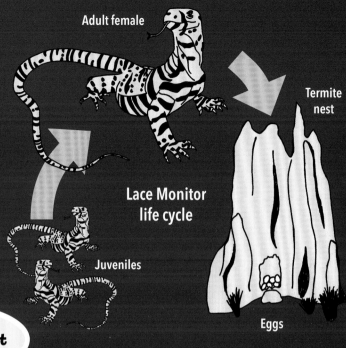

Adult female

Termite nest

Lace Monitor life cycle

Juveniles

Eggs

The hatchlings are exact replicas of their parents, and once emerged from their nest they do not require any parental care.

Threats

Sadly, in many parts of eastern Australia, baby Lace Monitors are quickly eaten by feral cats and foxes. Scientists believe that there is very little recruitment of babies growing up into adulthood in many populations, which has very serious consequences for the survival of this magnificent lizard species in some parts of Australia.

Lace Monitors often fall victim to vehicle strike, as they frequently sunbake on roads to thermoregulate.

Loss of habitat, land clearing and habitat fragmentation threaten many populations of this lizard in the southern parts of its range. Timber collection for firewood destroys the home of this prehistoric-looking lizard.

Land clearing in many parts of south-eastern Australia destroys the termite mounds where this lizard lays its eggs.

SCAN HERE
to watch a WILD clip

ogatim

Jungle Carpet Python

Morelia spilota cheynei

'Let's meet one of my favourite Australian snakes. A smaller rainforest subspecies of the Carpet Python... the Jungle Carpet Python.'

What's in a name?

Genus **Morelia** – a city in Mexico, also a girl's name. The species name **spilota** means spotted. Subspecies **cheynei** – named after a person.

> Snakes don't have a chin bone like you and I do.

Classification

KINGDOM: Animalia
PHYLUM: Chordata
CLASS: Reptilia
ORDER: Squamata
FAMILY: Pythonidae
GENUS: *Morelia*
SPECIES: *spilota*
SUBSPECIES: *cheynei*

Where is it found?

A tree-loving denizen of far north Queensland tropical rainforests. Although non-venomous, this snake is armed with backwards-curved sharp teeth for latching onto its prey. They are often found near waterways and creeks. In many parts of Australia Carpet Pythons are welcome visitors living in human dwellings such as homes, sheds and barns, since they help to control rat populations.

Amazing morphology and adaptations

Carpet pythons don't hop, skip or jump – they slither, using their muscles and scales to grip surfaces and propel themselves along.

They have the ability to eat huge prey items, many times larger than their own heads. Their lower jaw is not fused, instead it's held together by flexible muscles and ligaments. This enables the snake to stretch its lower jaw out incredibly wide.

Nostril

Eye

Teeth

As hatchlings and juveniles, this snake preys on lizards and small mammals. As they grow larger their diet is ever expanding, predating upon possums, bandicoots and birds.

Jungle Carpet Pythons have a muscular and flexible prehensile tail. They use it to grab on as they climb.

Jungle Carpet Pythons have a reputation of being rather 'flighty' and aggressive compared to their other Carpet Python cousins.

Their exceptional camouflage is perfect for hiding in sun-dappled environments beneath the tree canopy. Often covered in darker blotches and splotches, their colouration assists them in heating up more quickly in the sun. Even tropical rainforests can be cool at times.

It's kind of like a hand... or a monkey's tail for hanging on.

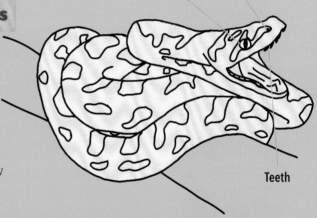

Producing copious amounts of saliva helps the Jungle Carpet Python to ingest its food, lubricating its prey and making it slippery to swallow. It can take hours to swallow a large animal.

Now that really is playing with your food.

Highly acrobatic in nature, they are equally at home slithering through the tree canopy, or on the rainforest floor.

Using their forked tongue, they have an exceptional sense of smell that helps them when searching for food.

The large heat-sensory pits alongside their mouth assist them in locating warm-blooded food, detecting the infrared heat of birds and mammalian quarry.

These powerful snakes use their strong muscles to overpower and asphyxiate their prey.

The amazing thing about snakes is that they are cold-blooded or ectothermic, which means that they receive most of their bodily energy from their external environment.

Hey that's amazing – that is one cheap energy bill.

They wrap around your neck… stop you from breathing, and then swallow you whole.

Carpet pythons can survive on 10 meals a year.

That's incredible... I think that I would surely have a grumbly tummy.

Snakes do such a great job for people. They eat up all of the mice and rats. That's great for me, as the only animal that I'm petrified of is rodents – **EEEEEEEEKK!** If I saw a mouse or rat... I would jump up on a chair and scream out for my **MUM**.

When disturbed, the Jungle Carpet Python will make a loud hiss. If a would-be intruder or attacker doesn't 'stand-down' this snake will not hesitate to strike out and attack. If captured, it will writhe around wildly and defecate on its captor. The powerful stench of its 'poo' does not disappear easily.

Many people throughout the world understandably fear snakes. However, once you get to know our serpentine friends, you can't help but fall in love with them, and they really don't mean us any harm.

> **Wow... that's much cheaper and more eco-friendly than buying clothes.**

Jungle Carpet Pythons don't have to go to the shops to buy their clothes, when they grow larger, their old skin peels off, making a new shiny one underneath.

All snakes lack eyelids, so when they are about to shed their skin, their eyes become milky and opaque. This is because they also shed their eye scale/shield at this time. Just before shedding they can become rather aggressive as they can't see, and they may strike out at any movement.

Life cycle

All python species lay eggs. The female Jungle Carpet Python employs maternal incubation of her eggs, protectively coiling around them during the incubation process. Carpet Pythons have the ability to shiver, vibrating their muscles to keep the eggs warm. The baby snakes can take up to 60 days to incubate. The female python will not eat during this time. Once hatched, the baby pythons have to fend for themselves. They are easy prey for goannas, kookaburras and owls.

Threats

Jungle Carpet Pythons often fall victim to traffic as they slither across roads. Habitat fragmentation, loss of habitat and household pets are also serious threats to this stunning snake.

Remember, next time you stumble across a snake in the wild, look but don't disturb, and marvel at one of nature's truly amazing creatures.

It's illegal to kill any snake in Australia – they are all protected species.

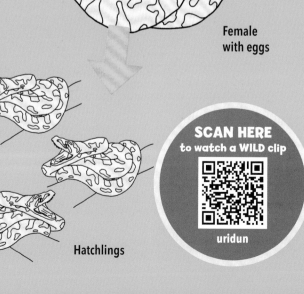

Female with eggs

Hatchlings

SCAN HERE
to watch a WILD clip

uridun

31

Eastern Long-necked Turtle

Chelodina longicollis

'What is the difference between a turtle and a tortoise?
I'm glad that you asked.
Tortoises are land-based (terrestrial) and have walking feet, whereas turtles have swimming feet and are aquatic, which means that they live in the water.'

What's in a name?

The name of the order **Testudines** is derived from the Latin 'testa' meaning shell. The genus name **Chelodina** means 'land turtle' and the species name ***longicollis*** means 'having a long neck.'

Classification

KINGDOM: Animalia
PHYLUM: Chordata
CLASS: Reptilia
ORDER: Testudines
FAMILY: Chelidae
GENUS: *Chelodina*
SPECIES: *longicollis*

Where is it found?

Eastern Long-necked Turtles are found in freshwater ecosystems along the east and south coasts of Australia, ranging from Queensland, through New South Wales and Victoria, to the south-east of South Australia.

In Australia there are no naturally occurring tortoises. There are only freshwater turtles, which generally have webbed feet for swimming, and ocean turtles, which have flippers.

Eastern Long-necked Turtles are semi-aquatic, and inhabit freshwater rivers, lakes, ponds and dams. They also like to spend time sunbaking on river banks and exposed logs. After heavy rains, Eastern Long-necked Turtles often search out new environments to live in, which might have more space and food.

Amazing morphology and adaptations

These turtles are carnivorous in nature, hunting for worms, insects, tadpoles, fish, yabbies and other aquatic invertebrates. Scientists have discovered that freshwater turtle species are vital for the health of river systems and waterways. Why? Because they act as environmental cleaners by consuming dead organisms, which helps to prevent the waterways becoming polluted and deoxygenated.

WOW, they are nature's garbage collectors.

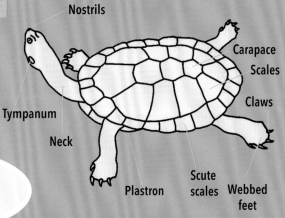

Nostrils

Carapace

Scales

Claws

Tympanum

Neck

Scute scales

Plastron

Webbed feet

Sometimes referred to as the 'stinker,' if disturbed or captured they are famous for emitting a noxious foul stench from their **cloaca** and 'arm-pits.' This smell is an attempt to dissuade would-be predators from eating them.

YUK... That's disgusting.

The long neck is perfect for darting out and ambushing prey.

That's one **looooooong** neck!

The top part of their shell is called the **carapace**, and the bottom part is called the **plastron**. All together it serves as great protection from attack by predators.

Hey, they don't have any bills or rent... they are always on holidays. **What a life.**

The Eastern Long-necked Turtle's nose is placed at the top of the head... perfect for an aquatic lifestyle. They are able to breathe as they swim beneath the water, so it's a bit like a built-in snorkel.

The turtle's ears are covered by a flap of skin called a tympanum, which stops water and foreign objects entering the ear canal whilst they swim.

That's very clever – they don't have to wear ear-plugs when they go to the swimming pool.

Perfectly adapted for swimming, they have webbed feet – that's skin between their fingers and toes which acts like built-in flippers.

The outside of the shell is covered in scute scales which are highly vascularised with lots of fine blood vessels. The large scales assist in heating up their cold blood (ectothermic bodies) in the sun.

That's like built-in solar panels.

Sometimes they feign death by sitting very still.

The plastron is usually brightly coloured, just like a black-and-yellow bumblebee. These warning colours potentially scare off predators.

It's kind of like a built-in 'Stop' sign!

The best way to hold a freshwater turtle is to imagine that you're holding a sandwich or a cheeseburger.

Place your hands from behind – one directly on top and the other directly underneath. This technique will avoid being scratched by their powerful sharp-clawed limbs.

If these turtles ever find themselves stuck on their back, or carapace, they can use their long strong necks to flip themselves back over again.

Young Eastern Long-necked Turtles have bright red-and-black plastrons. This colour fades as they grow bigger.

Life cycle

Eastern Long-necked Turtles are highly **polygamous**, which means that the male has more than one girlfriend. Turtles are oviparous, which means that they reproduce by laying hard-shelled eggs on land. The female can lay a clutch of up to 24 eggs in a nest, which she digs into soft sand or soil.

Baby turtles are called hatchlings, and can take up to 150 days to incubate and hatch from an egg. The baby turtles are fully independent when they hatch, receiving no parental care.

Female Eastern Long-necked Turtles usually grow bigger than the males. They can be as long as 28cm.

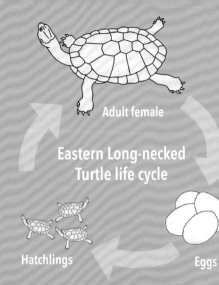

Adult female

Eastern Long-necked Turtle life cycle

Hatchlings

Eggs

Eastern Long-necked Turtles often move from their water body after downpours of rain. Sadly, they fall victim to car strike as they cross our busy roads and freeways. If you see a turtle crossing a road, always stop and help them on their way.

Did you know that some Australian turtles have the ability to absorb oxygen through their highly vascularised cloaca.

**Who would have thought it?
A bum-breathing turtle!**

Threats

Freshwater turtle species throughout Australia are on the decline. Although, seemingly common and often observed, hatchling baby turtles are quickly gobbled up by a swag of predators such as kookaburras, water rats, egrets, sea-eagles, goanna lizards and even large fish, and also introduced predators such as the Red Fox and feral cats. Scientific studies have recently discovered that, alarmingly, there is very little recruitment of baby turtles back into their natural environment. Once the adult turtles die out, the populations of all freshwater turtle species are under serious threat of extinction.

Our plastic waste negatively impacts freshwater turtle species throughout the world. Plastic bottle rings can easily trap and ensnare turtles. Turtles have also been known to ingest our plastic waste, causing death.

SCAN HERE
to watch a WILD clip

asozul

Saltwater Crocodile

Crocodylus porosus

'Meet the largest living reptile on Earth.'

What's in a name?

Crocodylus is derived from the Greek word **krokodeilos**, which literally means '**pebble-worm**.' The species name *porosus* means 'full of callosities,' referring to the sensory pores on the tip of their snout which are used for detecting electrical impulses emitted by their prey.

Osteoderms

Eyes

Nose

Tail/scutes

Webbed back feet

Legs

Teeth

Classification

KINGDOM:	Animalia
PHYLUM:	Chordata
CLASS:	Reptilia
ORDER:	Crocodilia
FAMILY:	Crocodylidae
GENUS:	*Crocodylus*
SPECIES:	*porosus*

Where is it found?

Saltwater Crocodiles are not only found in Australia, but also India, Sri Lanka, throughout South-East Asia, the Philippines, Indonesia and Papua New Guinea. In Australia they occur in northern tropical coastal areas from Broome in the west to Gladstone in south-east Queensland.

WARNING: Don't be fooled by their name – they can travel great distances inland, residing in freshwater ecosystems as well. Do not swim in a crocodile's territory. You will end up as **LUNCH!**

Amazing morphology and adaptations

Capable of growing to more than 6 metres in length, the largest Saltwater Crocodile ever recorded was a **WHOPPING** 8.63 metres! It was nicknamed **'Krys' The Savannah King** and hunted and killed in Normanton, Queensland. Although some scientists dispute the authenticity of these measurements, I reckon it's definitely possible.

Saltwater Crocodiles are gender dimorphic, which means that the male and female are different in size. In the case of this species, the males are much larger and can weigh up to 1,000kg.

As adults, Saltwater Crocodiles are top-order apex predators, which means that they eat everything else. In Australia Saltwater Crocodiles were hunted to the brink of extinction in the 1960s. Now they are fully protected and have rebounded remarkably in most of their range. However, in many parts of populated Queensland, habitat destruction and persecution from people has made them a rare species to this day.

Saltwater Crocodiles have a transparent sidewards-moving eyelid called a **nictitating membrane**, which allows them to see beneath the water when swimming.

Wow, that's like a built-in pair of goggles.

I wonder if they have a crocodile tooth fairy... they'd be pretty busy!

They can have more than 60 teeth in their mouths, which perfectly interlock to grab their prey. Voracious predators, their teeth frequently fall out, but are constantly replenished by replacement teeth. Humans only get two sets of teeth in their lives, whereas crocodiles' teeth grow back again and again.

Their strong powerful tail helps to propel them through the water at a surprising speed, even enabling them to vertically leap out of the water to 'snatch' their prey.

Webbed feet assist these reptiles to be highly efficient swimmers. They have claws on their toes to help them to grip on and climb out on slippery muddy river banks.

Saltwater Crocodiles are covered in impressive body-armour scales called **osteoderms** (meaning 'bony-skin'), which protect them from attack by predators when young, as well as from other crocodiles when fighting for food and territory.

Saltwater Crocodiles have long streamlined bodies, with eyes, ears and nostrils perfectly placed on top of their heads.

It's a perfect design for an aquatic predator – it can close off its ears and nostrils when diving and swimming.

This crocodile's tongue doesn't move like our tongue does. Instead its tongue has a membrane attached to the roof of the mouth so that it doesn't move. Alligators can poke their tongues out, whereas Saltwater Crocodiles cannot.

Stealth predators, they lie motionless on the edge of the water, with the intention of ambushing unsuspecting prey.

Saltwater Crocodiles possess salt glands which enable them to live in and drink saltwater.

Their cousins, the alligators and caimans, do not possess this adaptation.

What's the difference between an alligator and a crocodile? It's all in the teeth! When the jaws are closed, alligators' lower teeth are hidden in jaw sockets, whereas crocodiles' upper and lower teeth usually interlock, and are visible.

Alligators' mouths are shorter and more u-shaped, whereas Saltwater Crocodiles have a 'pointier' snout for grabbing a greater variety of prey items.

Scientists have studied the closing jaw pressure of a Saltwater Crocodile and gauged it at 3,700 PSI (pounds per square inch). To put that power into perspective, people have a jaw pressure between 150–200 PSI.

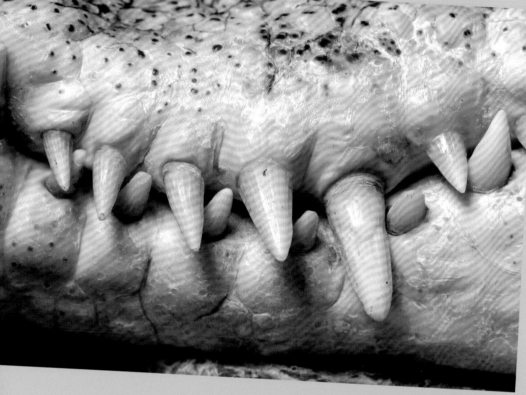

Saltwater Crocodiles don't chew their food – they swallow it in huge pieces. They employ a unique adaptation of swallowing stones to assist in grinding and crushing food items in their stomach. Combined with powerful acidic stomach juices, Saltwater Crocodiles are one frightfully efficient killing machine.

These top apex predators are incredibly adaptive, and they have outlasted the dinosaurs, with very little change in appearance for the past 180 million years. It's safe to say that these remarkable animals have perfected their body design.

Ambush predators, once their prey is taken, they'll drag their dinner down under the water and 'death-roll.' This involves spinning wildly, often hitting their prey violently on objects to knock it unconscious. Saltwater Crocodiles will hold their prey beneath the water until it drowns. The crocodile is able to survive as it has a **palatal valve** at the back of the mouth which stops water entering the airway.

Life cycle

Saltwater Crocodiles are oviparous, which means that they lay eggs to reproduce. In Australia, these giant reptiles breed in the wet season between October and May. The female constructs a nest by scraping together decomposing vegetation to build a mound, and then digs a small egg chamber in the top. The female can lay up to 60 hard-shelled eggs, and once laid, she covers them with vegetation. The incubation period usually lasts 2–3 months. The eggs stay warm from the heat of the sun and the rotting vegetation.

Adult male

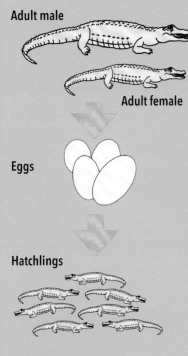

Adult female

Eggs

Hatchlings

The female remains close to the nest, defending her eggs from predators. Amazingly, the gender of the young is determined by the incubation temperature. If the eggs fall below 26–28°C for too long, the embryos can die or be born with deformities. Ideally the temperature should be around 30–32°C. Warmer temperatures normally produce male offspring, whereas cooler temperatures generally produce females.

When the young hatch, they break out of their eggs with a tiny egg tooth on the tip of their snout. The protective mother helps dig out the young from the nest, and will carry them to the safety of the water in her mouth. She'll continue to aggressively protect them for a short while afterwards.

It is thought that crocodiles can live beyond 100 years, perhaps even older.

Threats

Adult Saltwater Crocodiles have few natural predators. However, juveniles can be predated by birds such as sea-eagles, large fish, turtles and even larger crocodiles. Whilst incubating, the eggs can be eaten by marauding goannas and pigs.

Saltwater Crocodiles are regarded as endangered across much of their world range. They face many human threats, with pollution of waterways, hunting and habitat degradation among the huge factors which threaten the 'king' of all reptiles.

SCAN HERE
to watch a WILD clip

egozic

Green Tree Frog

Litoria caerulea

'Probably the most commonly kept frog pet in the world.'

What's in a name?

The Green Tree Frog is known as the 'dunny frog' in many parts of Australia, as it often seeks refuge in human toilets to escape the harsh desiccating heat. It is also known as the White's Tree Frog and the 'dumpy frog'.

The genus name **Litoria** means 'tree frog'. The species name *caerulea* means 'blue,' and it was reported that the first-ever Green Tree Frog specimen sent from Australia to museum collections in Europe was preserved in alcohol, causing the pigments in the skin of the frog to turn blue, hence the name.

Classification

KINGDOM:	Animalia
PHYLLUM:	Chordata
CLASS:	Amphibia
ORDER:	Anura
FAMILY:	Pelodryadidae
GENUS:	*Litoria*
SPECIES:	*caerulea*

Where is it found?

One of the largest and most widespread frogs in Australia. Green Tree Frogs are widely distributed up the east coast of Australia from north of Sydney, across inland areas and through tropical northern parts of Australia. They are still relatively common across most of their range.

Green Tree Frogs are nocturnal, and are most active on warm humid nights.

Green Tree Frogs can drink through their skin like a sponge – **SLUUUURRP!**

Amazing morphology and adaptations

Frogs are of course amphibians. They have glandular skin which can absorb moisture and oxygen. Frog species throughout the world are extremely sensitive to human pollution, litter and waste.

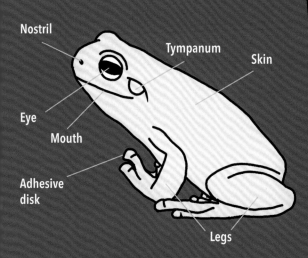

Nostril

Tympanum

Skin

Eye

Mouth

Adhesive disk

Legs

Although they have very plump, round bodies, and short robust arms and legs, Green Tree Frogs are excellent climbers. At the end of each toe they have round adhesive discs to help them grip, climb and leap. They can even climb up glass.

The adhesive discs are made up of tiny grooves like a human fingerprint, from which they secrete a sticky mucus to help them to climb. Spiderman, eat your heart out!

They can wee all over you like a frog water pistol... in the hope that you don't eat them.

Their colouration affords these frogs fantastic camouflage to hide from predators such as birds, lizards and snakes. Green Tree Frogs can vary in colour from bright green to brown depending on environmental conditions.

The Green Tree Frog is an incredibly adaptive species, often living in human dwellings, toilets and drain pipes. Interestingly enough, Green Tree Frogs **LOVE** to croak in drain pipes as it amplifies the sound, helping them to call out to potential mates.

Their ears are covered by a membrane of skin called a **tympanum**, which seals their ear so water doesn't enter the ear canal.

It's a bit like a loud speaker.

No need for ear plugs when you go swimming.

55

They also like to hang out near human-made fluorescent lights at night, because these are very attractive to all manner of bugs.

That's a very clever behavioural adaptation – it's like a frog restaurant.

When attacked, Green Tree Frogs emit a loud scream. This defence mechanism will hopefully deter any would-be attacker. If that doesn't work, they have been known to squirt water (wee!) out of their backside (cloaca) and urinate all over potential danger.

Green Tree Frogs shed their outer skin layer every few days or so.

They don't flick their discarded skin in the bin... they eat it. YU**K!** Waste not, want not in the animal kingdom.

Green Tree Frogs do a great job for us – they eat up all of the bugs. However, larger specimens can eat mice, lizards, snakes and even insectivorous bats.

These remarkable amphibians do not keep their eyes open whilst eating, and they use their eye-balls to assist in pushing large food items down their throat. **WOW WOW WOW!**

Green Tree Frogs are capable acrobatic jumpers – they can leap over one metre. They are highly flexible with their bodies as their bones are flexible and hollow, meaning that they can sustain falls from high places while avoiding injury.

Frogs are so important for the food chain. Not only do they help us out by eating up all of the pesky insects and arthropods – they are an important prey item for many different species.

Did you know that the Green Tree Frog has been highly studied by the medical world? In fact scientists have studied the antibacterial and antiviral properties of frog-skin secretions and have been able to synthesise drugs which assist people.

Only the male Green Tree Frog croaks.

They don't go 'Laaa-deee-daah-dee-dah' or 'Galump-Galump…' they go '**CRAAAAWK… CRAAAAAWK CRAAAAWK.**'

Life cycle

Green Tree Frogs lay their eggs in water bodies. They are not fussy, and have even been known to lay their eggs in plant pots. Green Tree Frogs are **oviparous**, and the female can lay up to 2,000 eggs. Once laid it only takes three days for the eggs to hatch into tadpoles. Green Tree Frog tadpoles are **aquatic** and live in water – they have a round head, eyes, tiny side fins, gills for absorbing oxygen from the water, and a long tail for swimming. As they grow, the tadpole must undergo **metamorphosis**. They gradually grow their back and their front legs. When they have all four legs and a long tail, they are called a froglet. At this stage, they develop lungs for breathing air and they reabsorb their long tail. This developmental process can take around six weeks.

Green Tree Frogs are long-lived amphibians. This species has been recorded to live for more than 40 years in captivity.

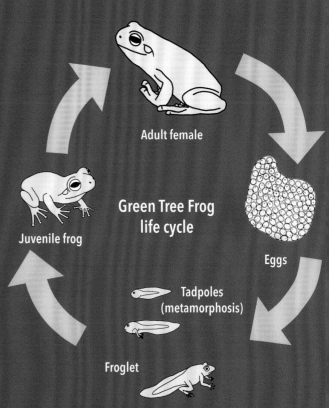

Green Tree Frog life cycle

Adult female

Eggs

Tadpoles (metamorphosis)

Froglet

Juvenile frog

I found a Green Tree Frog sticking to the public toilets when I was a kid… his name is Freddo… we have been best friends ever since… I still have him to this day.

Threats

The introduced Cane Toad outcompetes native frog species and poisons their eggs and tadpoles when they deposit eggs in the same water body.

One of the biggest threats to this gorgeous frog is loss of suitable habitat and shelter.

Domestic pets such as cats and dogs will predate on this species.

Green Tree Frogs are poisonous to your pets. When stressed they exude a substance over their skin which can cause vomiting.

Human pollution and waste in waterways negatively affects Green Tree Frogs. The chemicals in herbicides and pesticides also kill frog species.

Frogs worldwide have been decimated by a fungal disease called chytrid fungus, which attacks their skin.

SCAN HERE
to watch a WILD clip

aviges

61

Tawny Frogmouth

Podargus strigoides

'Many Australians mistakenly think that this bird is an owl.'

What's in a name?

Podargus means **'gouty'** and *strigoides* means **'owl-like bird.'**

Classification

KINGDOM: Animalia
PHYLUM: Chordata
CLASS: Aves
ORDER: Caprimulgiformes
FAMILY: Podargidae
GENUS: *Podargus*
SPECIES: *strigoides*

Where is it found?

Tawny Frogmouths are distributed across mainland Australian and Tasmania. Although they are not commonly found in the arid interior, they are still present in smaller numbers.

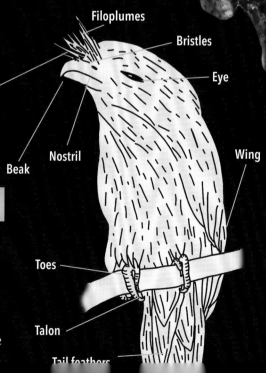

Filoplumes
Bristles
Eye
Tufts
Nostril
Beak
Wing
Toes
Talon
Tail feathers

Amazing morphology and adaptations

t's a common mistake in Australia to call them an owl. These birds are in fact close cousins to nightjars, and belong to the order Caprimulgiformes, which is Latin for goat-sucker.' Erroneously, in the past this family of birds was thought to have drunk the milk of goats. They have a huge, wide, gaping gob to catch insects on the wing. These birds have 'soft' feet for perching, and don't have large

Frogmouths are often found around human habitation at night-time, because they love to eat up all of the insects which are attracted to bright lights.

It's an easy way to get a free feed! That's their ecological niche – they eat up all of the bugs – so that's why we need to look after them.

Check out these sensory feathers on the top part of their head – these are for detecting bugs whilst on the wing. They use their wide-open mouth to catch their prey – just like a huge net to trap their food.

Tawny Frogmouths have a third eyelid. It's called a nictitating membrane and it helps keep their eyes clean from dust and dirt.

They don't need to use a face-washer... how about that?

Have a good look at their fabulous camouflage, which they use when hiding motionless in the daytime on a dead tree branch.

They eat insects, arthropods, small reptiles, small birds, and even frogs.

Tawny Frogmouths are nocturnal – they have large eyes for seeing in the dark.

They have a very curious defence mechanism. If they get attacked by a would-be predator they poo in its face! **Pooooooooweee**.

If that doesn't work, they open their wide gaping bright yellow mouth to frighten an attacker.

For a relatively small bird they have an enormously large beak. To make sure that they don't topple over with the weight of such a large bill, the bottom part is made up of a frame with skin stretched across... kind of like a pelican's beak.

Tawny Frogmouths have powdery down feathers. They shed a fine waxy powder that coats and waterproofs their feathers.

Hey, they don't have to wear a rain jacket.

Tawny Frogmouths are experts at adapting to Australia's extreme weather conditions. In the colder winter months they can shut down their energy requirements by going into a state of torpor, so that they can cope with the loss of energy and heat. In the hot summer months they produce a mucus in their mouths, and when they inhale and exhale rapidly it cools down their body.

That's like built-in air conditioning.

Life cycle

When breeding, Tawny Frogmouths lay their two or three eggs in the 'flimsiest' of nests. They have a reputation in the 'bird world' of being a very bad nest-builder – almost as bad as doves and pigeons.

Male Tawny Frogmouths are fiercely defensive of their nest and their mate, aggressively fending off intruders. These birds are monogamous and they mate for life. Their chicks are among the cutest of all birds – they look like little fluff balls.

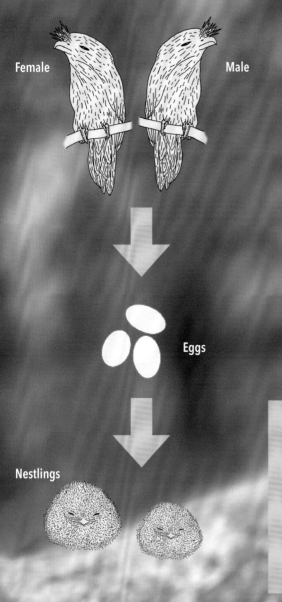

Female   Male

Eggs

Nestlings

Threats

Nocturnal in habit, these birds sadly get struck by vehicles at night-time. They chase the insects which are attracted by the automobile headlights.

Tawny Frogmouths have adapted well to life in urban areas. However, disappointingly people choose to let their cats roam freely. People's domestic pets such as cats and dogs see Tawny Frogmouths as easy prey. Remember to always keep your pet cat enclosed, so it doesn't eat our native wildlife.

Loss of habitat is a continual threat for this species, as they need old mature eucalyptus trees to nest in. Their flimsily built nests are not suitable for young trees.

Ingestion of toxins through eating poisoned vermin such as rodents and insects can kill these beautiful birds. We all need to make our environments a safe place for our native wildlife to live in. After all, they were here first.

Baby Tawny Frogmouths spend up to 31 days as nestlings, before become fledglings. The fluffy hatchlings are semi-altricial, and have closed eyes and need care from their parents. Fledglings disperse within a month of leaving the nest and will reproduce themselves at around one year of age.

SCAN HERE
to watch a WILD clip

akesel

Barn Owl
Tyto alba

'These silent nocturnal hunters are ace at pest control.'

What's in name?

Tyto is a generic Greek (Latin) name for 'owl,' **alba** is a Latin word meaning 'white'

Classification

KINGDOM:	Animalia
PHYLUM:	Chordata
CLASS:	Aves
ORDER:	Strigiformes
FAMILY:	Tytonidae
GENUS:	*Tyto*
SPECIES:	*alba*

Where is it found?

The Barn Owl is one of the most easily recognised and widespread owls in the world, found on every continent except Antarctica. In Australia it is found across the entire country. Barn Owls in Australia prefer to nest in tree hollows, whereas their cousins in other parts of the world often nest in structures made by humans.

Amazing morphology and adaptations

Barn Owls are best identified by their heart-shaped facial disc.

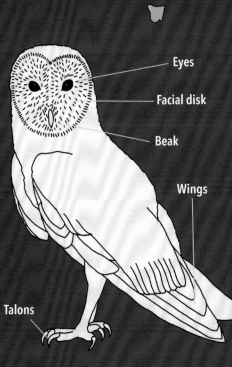

Eyes

Facial disk

Beak

Wings

Talons

Their round face helps them to funnel sound towards their ears, which are located just behind their eyes. Amazingly, their left ear is lower than their right ear, helping them to triangulate the sources of sounds and pinpoint exactly where their prey is located.

Hey, that's like 3D listening.

71

Their large black eyes help them to see at night. They are forward facing, giving them excellent depth perception and incredible vision in low light levels. They can spin their heads around 270°.

Like something in a horror movie!

Barn Owls have 14 vertebrae in their necks – more than human beings. This helps them to pivot their necks, which is a great adaptation when their eyes cannot move in their skull.

They have mostly white feathers on their undersides, with pale grey to pale brown colouring on their wings and back and on the top of the head. Barn Owls have perfect camouflage for hiding undetected within the tree canopy.

Barn Owls are known as **raptors**, and are equipped with sharp powerful talons on their feet for capturing their prey, which they swoop down onto and grab. The speed and force of their attack often breaks the neck or back of their unsuspecting victim and kills it instantly.

These owls have very long legs, to help them reach their prey through undergrowth such as long grass.

Their scimitar-shaped beak is relatively long and curved – it is designed for tearing strips of flesh off their food.

They can't use a knife and fork when they are eating.

They cannot chew their food, so they swallow pieces of prey whole, including feathers, bone and fur. Later, they regurgitate a pellet containing all the items which they can't digest. **YUK!**

Barn Owls are silent hunters of the night. Their incredibly soft feathers are uniquely structured and arranged, which allows air to pass over them soundlessly and absorbs most noise from their flapping wings.

Barn Owls are commonly found in open spaces, including farmlands and forests with grassy understorey for prey to occupy. Hunting and feeding at night, they predate upon small mammals such as rodents, small possums, reptiles and amphibians.

The male hunts and captures food for the female whilst she is incubating the eggs. Both parents share parental duties in hunting for food for their ever-hungry, rapidly growing chicks. It takes 10–13 weeks before the young Barn Owls will be fully fledged and able to fly.

This remarkably successful owl species matures at around 12 months of age, when it will commence breeding and start raising a family.

Adult

Tree hollow nest

Chick

Life cycle

Barn Owls are generally monogamous, which means that they usually mate for life.

This owl is known as a 'boom and bust' species, and its breeding season is dependent on prey availability and plentiful seasons. They have the ability to produce multiple clutches of young when food is abundant.

The female alone incubates the eggs in the nest, which is usually located in a tree hollow. Barn Owls lay between three and six eggs, and each egg is laid two days apart. The young owls hatch days apart as well, and vary dramatically in size as they grow in the nest. If the prey supply diminishes it is not uncommon for smaller chicks to be killed and fed to older larger chicks.

Did you know that a baby owl chick is known as an owlet?

Threats

Barn Owls have a high mortality in their first year of life. Life in Australia is certainly tough. Food can often be scarce and the young owls struggle to find enough to eat whilst still perfecting their hunting techniques. Barn Owls have adapted for these extreme conditions by having large broods of young, so that they can rapidly increase their numbers when food is plentiful.

Sadly, Barn Owls are often hit by vehicles on our busy roads.

So, keep a look out for them when driving at night-time.

People often use rodenticides and poisons to control and eradicate mice and rats around human habitation. Unfortunately, Barn Owls often fall victim to secondary poisoning when they eat sick or dead rodents.

Did you know that Barn Owls never hoot like owls do in the movies – instead they let out a piercing shriek.

A wild Barn Owl can eat up to four mice in an evening meal. We need more Barn Owls because they really help people out. Imagine your neighbourhood without Barn Owls living nearby – there would be mice and rats everywhere.

That would be my worst nightmare.

What can we all do to help Barn Owls?

We can erect nest boxes in our local areas, creating roosting and nesting sites. Stop using rodenticides to control vermin, and simply welcome Barn Owls to live in your area.

SCAN HERE
to watch a WILD clip

ucerul

Laughing Kookaburra

Dacelo novaeguineae

Classification

KINGDOM:	Animalia
PHYLUM:	Chordata
CLASS:	Aves
ORDER:	Coraciiformes
FAMILY:	Halcyonidae
GENUS:	Dacelo
SPECIES:	*novaeguineae*

'Australia's bush alarm clock!'

What's in name?

Dacelo is an anagram of the Greek word *Alcedo*, meaning 'kingfisher,' while **novaeguineae** means 'of New Guinea.' In Australia the species is also referred to as the 'laughing jackass.'

Eye

Bro 'str

Beak

Talons

'Barred' tail feathers

Bl fea

Wings

78

Where is it found?

The Laughing Kookaburra is a very large tree-dwelling kingfisher species.

Instantly recognisable, this iconic bird is Australia's largest kingfisher species, and has adapted to drier ecosystems, where it is a highly successful carnivorous hunter. In fact, it is so successful that it has been introduced to parts of Western Australia, Tasmania and New Zealand, to eradicate pests. Unfortunately, due to the competitive nature of this bird, it has displaced many native bird species and has become a pest itself in some areas.

Amazing morphology and adaptations

The kookaburra often calls to welcome the dawn in the morning and sunset in the evening. It is quite possibly the most famous sound in the Australian bush. The Laughing Kookaburra's call was famously used in 'olden-day' Tarzan movies as background noise, even though kookaburras are not found in Africa.

Contrary to popular belief, the Laughing Kookaburra is far from being a 'happy-go-lucky' species. This bird's call is not one of mirth and merriment. The sound it makes is a territorial call to ward off competitors and other species from their territory.

The Laughing Kookaburra is highly social and gregarious and lives in tight-knit family groups which define their territory through delivering their song.

Basically saying, **BACK OFF**... if you come into our territory, you'll pay the price.

The loud 'koo-koo-koo-koo-kaa-kaa-kaa-kaa' is often sung in chorus with other family members.

Laughing Kookaburras require dead hollows in trees for nest sites. In many suburban areas of Australia, loss of suitable nest sites has been the cause of local reductions in kookaburra populations.

We need to do more to help them out.

Their relatively long and powerful bill is a perfect weapon for catching prey. A small venomous snake or blue-tongued lizard is no match for a hungry kookaburra. They are opportunistic feeders, eating yabbies, small birds, insects, mice and worms – even becoming quite brazen and stealing sausages off barbeques whilst people are still cooking.

Once caught, kookaburras violently **BASH** their prey against a tree branch to kill their victim, even if it's sausage!

'Chucky' the kookaburra hatched in my hand from an egg... so he thinks that I'm his dad. When I laugh, he laughs as well. It's pretty cool!

male Laughing
okaburras are
ghtly larger
size than the
les. Male
okaburras
nerally have
re blue on
eir rumps,
t above their
s. This is most
ticeable when
ey are in flight.
They sport a
nspicuous dark
own eye-stripe.

A bit like a **Zorro** mask

Laughing Kookaburras have excellent eyesight.
At any sign of movement they swoop down and
strike. They are one of the few birds in the world
which can hover.

Life cycle

The Laughing Kookaburra's success story pivots around family teamwork.

Offspring from the previous breeding season help their parents to raise the next clutch of chicks. They nest in tree hollows and abandoned termite nests in trees. The female can lay 1–5 eggs, and incubation lasts for 24–26 days. Kookaburra chicks fledge at around one month and fledglings will stay with the family group for one or two seasons before leaving to find a new territory. Juvenile kookaburras can be distinguished from adults as they have smaller beaks.

Kookaburras practice the brutal behaviour of siblicide whilst growing up in their nest. Although hatching blind and featherless, the babies are born with hooks on their beaks. They use these hooks to fight each other in the nest, often killing their smallest sibling. Only the strongest will survive. The dead baby is fed to hungry surviving siblings.

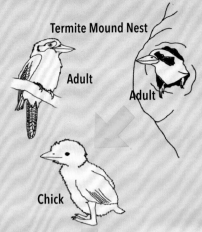

Termite Mound Nest

Adult

Adult

Chick

Juveniles

Now that's one tough way to start life.

Kookaburras are monogamous and mate for life, and both the male and female share egg incubation duties, as well as collecting food for their young.

Laughing Kookaburras can live up to 15 years in the wild, and even longer in captivity.

Sadly, young kookaburras fall victim to domestic household pets such as cats and dogs.

Laughing Kookaburras in many regions suffer from poisoning from insecticides and rodenticides made and spread by humans.

So be responsible pet owners - lock your cats up, and walk your dogs on a leash.

Keep your gardens clean from vermin, but don't use poisons.

In many built-up and suburban areas kookaburras have nowhere to lay their eggs, because mature trees with hollows have been removed to make way for human development.

SCAN HERE
to watch a WILD clip

Short-beaked Echidna

Tachyglossus aculeatus

'An Australian egg-laying mammal.'

What's in a name?

Tachyglossus means 'fast or quick tongue' and **aculeatus** means 'spiky.'

In the family name **Monotreme,** which relates to the echidna and platypus, 'mono' means 'one' and 'trema' means 'opening.'

The word **Echidna** is derived from a goddess in Greek mythology, who was known as the 'mother of all monsters.' She was half snake and half human. This name was influenced by the fact that although echidnas are warm-blooded mammals, they lay eggs like many reptiles.

Classification

KINGDOM:	Animalia
PHYLUM:	Chordata
CLASS:	Mammalia
ORDER:	Monotremata
FAMILY:	Tachyglossidae
GENUS:	*Tachglossus*
SPECIES:	*aculeatus*

Where is it found?

Short-beaked Echidnas are a real success story, being Australia's most widespread naturally occurring mammal, found in a diverse range of habitats and environments. They also live in southern New Guinea.

This is the only echidna species found in Australia. Although it walks with a distinctive waddling gait, the Short-beaked Echidna is a surprisingly efficient climber and swimmer.

Amazing morphology and adaptations

Echidnas are monotremes, and are the closest living relative of Australia's duck-billed Platypus. Like reptiles, these mammals have a single opening called a **cloaca**, through which bodily excrement is passed, while it is also the reproductive canal!

Echidnas can travel at up to 2.3km per hour, so they are not renowned for their speed!

Adult monotremes do not possess any teeth, and they don't have whiskers on their faces.

Short-beaked Echidnas have a long beak-like snout for snuffling through the undergrowth, and poking into rotting logs while hunting for their prey.

They have an excellent sense of smell. Echidnas hunt for insect larvae, ants, termites and earthworms. They slurp up their prey with their tongue which can be up to 18cm long. The tongue is covered with extremely sticky saliva which their prey adheres to.

Incredibly, the tip of their tongue can bend into a U-shape… and it can reach around corners inside ant mounds and termite colonies. Echidnas have been known to lick up 200 grams of ants in ten minutes.

Spines — Eye — Nostril — Claws — Beak — Tongue

When eating, Short-beaked Echidnas suck prey into their mouths, and it is crushed between horny pads on the back of their tongue and palate.

Woah... that's like a built-in vacuum cleaner.

In hotter months they remain in shelters during the day to avoid the heat, only venturing out at night to forage and feed.

Echidnas don't sweat.

Hey ... they don't have to wear deodorant!

Their back and tail are covered in spines, which
are modified hairs made of keratin. In between
these sharp spines is fur, which varies in density
depending on the climate in the region where
they live.

They have short powerful legs, with long claws on each foot.

Hind feet are pointing behind them, and they walk on top of their knuckles.

Short-beaked Echidnas do not have external ears. However, just like lizards and birds they have an opening on either side of their head. Echidnas' ears are large vertical slits located directly behind their eyes – they have excellent hearing.

Echidnas are curious animals as their front feet face forwards and their back feet face backwards. They have adapted to be able to dig down directly beneath themselves, in order to avoid danger and predation.

Short-beaked Echidnas are expert burrowers, and their powerful claws enable them to burrow completely underground very quickly. They can stay undetected for hours on end, as they have the ability to withstand higher levels of carbon dioxide and low oxygen levels. They are particularly well adapted for surviving raging bushfires – instead of running from the fire, they have been known to burrow deep below the surface for protection.

Their claws are specially shaped so that they can comb through their spines to reach their fur. It is thought that the echidna is host to the world's largest parasitic flea – the echidna flea.

Like an earthworks excavator!

Their limbs and claws are so powerfully strong that they can tear apart logs and move rocks much larger than themselves.

Echidnas have the second-lowest recorded body temperature of any mammal on the planet. Only the platypus has a lower body temperature. An active echidna body temperature is around 33°C, compared to 37°C in humans. Echidnas can go into a torpor over the cooler winter months in Australia. During this time they lower their metabolic rate and don't need to forage for food.

Echidna life cycle

Female

Egg

Puggle

Life cycle

When reproducing, the female echidna lays one leathery egg. The egg is placed in a rudimentary pouch (skin fold) on the female's underbelly. It only takes 10 days for the baby echidna to hatch – that is incredibly quick. A baby echidna is referred to as a 'puggle'. The puggle is born with powerful forearms and clings to hairs inside the pouch.

Echidnas' thick yellowish milk is extremely nutritious and full of energy. Echidnas do not have nipples for suckling. Instead, they drink from a specialised milk patch, with hundreds of pores which secrete milk.

The puggle grows quickly, and as its spikes begin to grow it is left in the burrow whilst the mother forages for food. Scientists have discovered that young echidnas in the nest can go for many days without eating. Young echidnas become independent at around six months of age.

Short-beaked Echidnas are surprisingly long-lived creatures, surviving up to 50 years in captivity.

Threats

Although not listed as endangered, echidna populations and numbers have been diminished in some areas of Australia due to fragmentation and loss of habitat. Their large home range and slow movement causes them to fall victim to car strike as they cross busy roads.

Adult echidnas have few predators. However, young echidnas are easy prey for dogs, cats, foxes, goannas and Wedge-tailed Eagles. Tasmanian Devils have been known to eat echidnas, spines and all!

Remember, always slow down when driving through echidna habitat, and always walk your dog on a lead.

SCAN HERE
to watch a WILD clip

okohil

Western Grey Kangaroo

Macropus fuliginosus

'Australia's big-foot.'

What's in name?

Makros means 'long' or 'large' and **pous** means 'feet,' while **fuliginosus** means 'sooty.'

Classification

KINGDOM:	Animalia
PHYLUM:	Chordata
CLASS:	Mammalia
ORDER:	Diprotodontia
FAMILY:	Macropodidae
GENUS:	*Macropus*
SPECIES:	*fuliginosus*

Where is it found?

The Western Grey Kangaroo is one of Australia's largest species of macropod. A relatively widespread and common species, it inhabits open woodlands, grasslands and semi-arid regions of southern parts of Australia. It is found from Shark Bay in Western Australia, across all of southern Australia, Victoria, the Murray-Darling Basin in New South Wales, and southern Queensland.

Western Grey Kangaroos have large ears for listening for approaching danger. They have white fur-lined ears, and dark-coloured extremities.

Kangaroos employ **pentapedal** locomotion, using all limbs and their huge tail to assist in forward motion. They can have five points of contact with the ground as they move. Kangaroos are the largest animals on earth that use energy-efficient hopping to bound. They can reach speeds of up to 64km per hour. Their long tail is like a 'tight-rope' pole for balance and changing direction.

The bottoms of a kangaroo's feet are covered in thick leathery skin, which protects them from sharp objects and the hard ground.

That's like a built-in pair of sneakers!

- Ears
- Nose
- Paws
- Claws
- Pouch
- Claws
- Feet
- Tail

Amazing morphology and adaptations

These kangaroos are masters of survival in Australia's harsh landscape. They can exist on nutrient-poor foods, eating grasses and foliage. They are generally herbivorous, but have been recorded eating carrion (dead flesh) to supplement their diets with protein.

Who would have thought!

They have sharp powerful claws on their hands for grabbing food, digging and fighting. This is one kangaroo you don't want to mess with.

To help them with grooming and scratching, their inside toes are fused together to make a syndactyl or grooming claw.

Western Grey Kangaroos are highly social, and live in large family groups called mobs. They usually socialise and come out to graze during dusk and dawn. Animals which come out at times of the day with low light levels are called **crepuscular**.

Kangaroos are very important for the Australian landscape. They are key grassland seed dispersers, ingesting seeds when they eat and pooping them out across barren landscapes. Their thick shaggy coat also transports many different Australian grass seeds and helps them to germinate elsewhere.

Kangaroos are a national emblem of Australia.

Life cycle

In the breeding season males often fight for dominance, so that they can mate with females.

Males stand up tall on their tails and kick out with their **HUGE** clawed feet at their opponent. To avoid serious injury, males have a large section of thick skin across their stomachs to protect their vital organs.

Kangaroos are mammals – they are **endothermic** (warm blooded), have fur-covered bodies, and they drink milk from their mother when they are young. They have an extremely short gestation period of approximately 30 days, giving birth to a tiny jelly bean-sized baby. Just before birth the mother licks a trail through her stomach fur, so that the baby can crawl its way into her pouch. The baby fuses to one of her two teats and suckles milk.

Western Grey Kangaroos are incredibly efficient at reproducing. Baby kangaroos are called joeys.

Adult female

Kangaroo life cycle

Joey

Pouch joey

They start hopping out of their mother's pouch and exploring the world at the age of nine months. Joey kangaroos are not fully weaned until they are approximately 18 months old.

Western Grey Kangaroos can live up to 20 years and grow as tall as 1.3 metres. There is a distinct difference in size between males and females. Females weigh as much as 34kg, whereas males can reach 70kg. Male Western Grey Kangaroos can be quite imposing and formidable animals.

Large male kangaroos are fearsome adversaries. When threatened or attacked they are more than capable of defending themselves. They have been known to attack and injure people, as well as drown dogs in dams when confronted.

In times of drought when there is a scarcity of food, or when threatened, female kangaroos will eject their baby joey to survive or escape from a hungry predator.

Threats

Although common across much of their range, Western Grey Kangaroos suffer from habitat loss and fragmentation, collisions with motor vehicles, and attacks from dogs and foxes.

With the advent of agriculture and increased open-water resources, Western Grey Kangaroos have rapidly increased in population in some areas, and sadly have become a pest species to farmers and are often shot.

If you live near wild kangaroo populations, slow down when driving around the hours of dusk and dawn, and remember to always walk your dog on a lead.

SCAN HERE
to watch a WILD clip

apajus

'Meet Australia's most iconic marsupial.'

Koala
Phascolarctos cinereus

Classification

KINGDOM:	Animalia
PHYLUM:	Chordata
CLASS:	Mammalia
ORDER:	Diprotodontia
FAMILY:	Phascolarctidae
GENUS:	*Phascolarctos*
SPECIES:	*cinereus*

What's in a name?

The Koala's scientific name is misleading. The genus name **Phascolarctos** means 'pouched-bear' and the species name **cinereus** means 'ash-grey.'

Amazing morphology and adaptations

Koalas belong to the class Mammalia – the mammals. This means that they have fur-covered bodies, they are endothermic (they heat up their bodies from within – also known as warm blooded) and they suckle milk from their mother during early development.

Of course, Koalas are not related to bears, they are in fact a pouched mammal, known as a marsupial.

Koalas have incredible adaptations for life in trees. They have strong muscular limbs with powerful claws, and two opposable thumbs for gripping onto branches and tree trunks.

Koalas have a hard cartilage plate on their back, which helps cushion their body whilst they are asleep against hard tree branches.

That's like a built-in cushion. Did you know that people's ears and nose are also made up of cartilage?

Where is it found?

Koalas inhabit tall open eucalyptus woodlands only on the eastern side of Australia. This gorgeous tree-loving marsupial isn't found anywhere else in the world. This makes it an endemic species, and one which we all need to treasure.

That certainly makes things confusing, because Koalas are not bears.

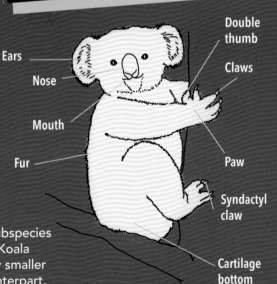

Ears
Nose
Mouth
Fur

Double thumb
Claws
Paw
Syndactyl claw
Cartilage bottom

There are two distinct subspecies of Koala – the Northern Koala subspecies is substantially smaller than its Southern Koala counterpart.

Koalas have incredible camouflage. Their grey-brown fur, dappled with specks of white, helps them to blend in amongst the tree canopy to avoid hungry predators.

Male Koalas have a large sweaty sternal gland on the front of their chest. They use this gland to rub onto trees and branches, marking where they live. This is to ward off potential male competition, and to advertise their presence to potential female mates.

Koala fur is dense and woolly, insulating it from extreme heat and cold. It also acts like a 'raincoat' to repel moisture when it rains.

Koalas have a fused double claw, which acts like a hairbrush to comb through their fur and to scratch out any itches.

Hey, they don't need to use a hairbrush!

It is the male Koala that usually bellows deeply, especially in the breeding season. They make a deep guttural sound that can be quite terrifying to the uninitiated. The noise they make is famous in 'Aussie' folklore.

Koalas can be active both day and night. This behaviour is known as being **cathemeral**.

Equipped with large fluffy ears, Koalas have exceptional hearing capabilities. They can move their ears independently, listening for approaching danger.

Koalas can easily defend themselves with their powerful claws, lashing out at danger.
    They move incredibly quickly if the need arises, and can readily bite.

Although there are around 900 different species of eucalyptus trees in Australia, koalas are incredibly fussy eaters, and have only been recorded to eat 40–50 species. Even then, geographically distinct Koala populations tend to only eat a handful of species in their particular region.
    Koalas use their huge 'boofy' noses to sniff and analyse the water content and toxicity of the food they are eating.

Koalas rarely drink water – they receive most of their fluid requirements by choosing the most succulent and moisture-rich leaves. These soft young leaves are known as 'tip.'

Koalas can eat up to 1kg of gum leaves a day. Eucalyptus leaves are very poor in nutritional value so a Koala must eat, then sleep, in order to efficiently digest its food. Koalas have been known to sleep up to 20 hours a day. Their large stomach, filled with masticated thinly sliced leaf-tips, is like a huge fermentation vat. Contrary to popular belief, Koalas are not drunk on gum leaves.

Because of their indigestible high-fibre diet, Koalas poop up to 200 times per day.

That's one regular Koala!

Life cycle

Baby Koalas – called joeys – drink milk from their mother's teat. The gestation period of a Koala is approximately 35 days, compared to a human's gestation period of nine months. The female Koala gives birth to a tiny baby the size of a jelly bean, which weighs only half a gram.

When born, the tiny undeveloped baby joey Koala crawls into the mother's backward-facing pouch, where it attaches to her teat to drink milk for sustenance. The mother's pouch is a perfect, warm, safe place to grow up and develop.

Adult female

Joey

Koala life cycle

Pouch joey

At nine months of age, the joey Koala has grown much bigger and can no longer easily fit inside the mother's pouch. Instead, it hangs on tight and 'piggy-backs' on the mother Koala's back. At 12 months of age, the joey Koala becomes independent and can look after itself, no longer requiring milk, and consumes gum leaves for breakfast lunch and tea.

> **How do they do this? They eat their mother's poo of course!**

The baby Koala stays in the mother's pouch for up to seven months, before it 'pops' its head out to inspect the world. At this stage of development it begins to slowly eat solid foods. But first the joey Koala must inoculate itself with bacteria, which aid it in digesting toxic gum leaves.

This specially prepared meal, called pap, is full of good bacteria which help Koalas to consume eucalyptus leaves. The baby joey Koala chows down on this delicious faecal concoction for about a month before it's able to start eating eucalyptus leaves.

This particular behaviour is called coprophagia.

Threats

The absolute biggest threat to Koalas today is loss of habitat. Although almost hunted to extinction for their fur pelts in the early 1900s, Koalas are fully protected by Federal Government law.

Sadly, where Koalas love to live, people love to live too. Urbanisation has destroyed Koala habitat and isolated it into small patches. Koalas fall victim to vehicle strike, climate change, bush fires, stress, disease and dog attack.

It is thought that less than 80,000 wild Koalas remain in their natural environment. Scientists predict that wild Koalas could become extinct by 2050.

SCAN HERE
to watch a WILD clip

iwodot

Grey-headed Flying-fox

Pteropus poliocephalus

'A refugee that desperately needs our help.'

They remind me of a flying Chihuahua!

Classification

KINGDOM:	Animalia
PHYLUM:	Chordata
CLASS:	Mammalia
ORDER:	Chiroptera
FAMILY:	Pteropodidae
GENUS:	*Pteropus*
SPECIES:	*poliocephalus*

Where is it found?

Grey-headed Flying-foxes occur along the east coast of Australia, from the central coast of Queensland to the south-eastern coast of South Australia. They occupy a range of forested habitats from mangrove forests along coastlines to wooded parks in urban areas.

Amazing morphology and adaptations

The Grey-headed Flying-fox is the largest bat in Australia – it can have a wingspan of up to one metre when outstretched. The common name of 'flying-fox' refers to the canine-like appearance of the head.

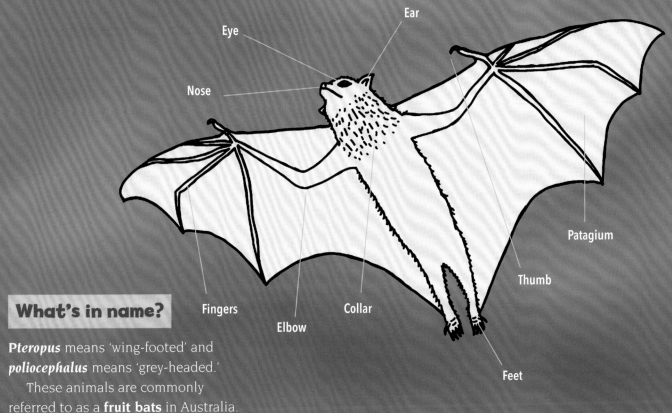

What's in name?

Pteropus means 'wing-footed' and **poliocephalus** means 'grey-headed.'
    These animals are commonly referred to as a **fruit bats** in Australia.

Grey-headed Flying-foxes
can fly hundreds of kilometres in one night.
This is so important, because they are such vital
pollinators of many Australian plant species.

The Grey-headed Flying-fox is known as a megabat, and is in a different family to the smaller insectivorous microbats. These 'fruit bats' are known as a **keystone species**, and are one of the most important animals in Australia.

The wings of a flying-fox are actually their hands.

Their long fingers extend to stretch out the flap of skin which is also attached to the ankles. This membrane of skin is called the patagium – the bat uses this to fly.

These bats eat fruit and pollen – they won't suck your blood!

As they fly around at night, flying-foxes poop out the seeds of the fruit which they have consumed, helping to revegetate the barren landscape.

Fruit bats are known as **frugivores**, which means that they love to eat fruit. Grey-headed Flying-foxes are responsible for cross-pollinating many of the eucalyptus hardwood forests which people rely on commercially for timber.

Their hairy bodies get dusted in pollen whilst feeding, and they effectively cross-pollinate other flowers at new feed sites.

115

Life cycle

Grey-headed Flying-foxes begin to breed at around two-and-a-half years of age. Their gestation period is approximately six months. They usually give birth to one well-developed baby whilst hanging upside-down. The female hangs on with her toes and thumbs to make a hammock with her body and catches the pup as it's born.

The newborn pup hangs on tightly for the first few weeks for protection and warmth, suckling milk from the mother's teat in her armpit, even when she is flying! The young pup will hitch a ride with its mum for six weeks or so. When big enough, the mother leaves her baby behind at the roosting site along with all of the other pups at the camp.

Mother

Pup 0–6 weeks

Flying fox life cycle

Mother

Pup 10–14 weeks

It's like a flying-fox kiddy creche!

Young flying-foxes start learning to fly at around 10–14 weeks. At six months of age, the young fruit bat becomes fully independent.

This species is gender dimorphic, meaning that the males are usually larger in size than the females. And the males can usually be visually distinguished from the females because they 'sport' a yellow nape, whereas females have a rusty-orange 'ginger' neck colour.

Unlike small insectivorous bats, flying-foxes do not use echolocation – instead they have large eyes enabling them to see well in the dark, and they have an excellent sense of smell.

Flying-foxes have thumb claws for grabbing onto branches whilst roosting.

They are like built-in ice-picks for hanging on.

They also have highly vascularised wings, intermeshed with fine blood-filled veins. When hot, this ingenious animal will flap its wings in the breeze to help cool itself down.

That is so clever – they don't need to turn on an expensive air conditioner.

Interestingly enough, when Grey-headed Flying-foxes are parasitised by lice and other ectoparasites, they don't need medicated shampoos from the chemist to eradicate the itchy unwelcome pests – they simply hang upside-down and wee on themselves. The uric acid in their urine eradicates these pests and cleans their furry coat.

What a clever idea.

In the day, Grey-headed Flying-foxes rest and squabble in mass conglomerations of up to 100,000 individuals. This noisy and most impressive mass gathering is called a 'camp' of bats. It is an extremely clever way to live, as 'safety in numbers' protects bats from the likelihood of attack from predators as they set off at dusk in search of food.

They sure know how to eat on the wing.

Flying long distances can be very tiring, and you don't want to be weighed down with a full belly of food. Grey-headed Flying-foxes have a very short digestive tract and they 'poo' out their digested food in under 20 minutes. This keeps them light enough for energy-efficient flying.

Threats

Grey-headed Flying-foxes must always be on the look-out for predators. Raptors, goannas and even pythons would love to devour a juicy fruit bat.

This species is listed as a vulnerable to extinction. Its population is rapidly declining due to loss of habitat, climate change and persecution by humans.

Grey-headed Flying-foxes live in many towns and cities in Australia, and are sadly seen as a pest, raiding peoples' backyards at night in search of scarce food. They often get trapped and die in fruit netting placed on trees.

SCAN HERE
to watch a WILD clip

aboqor

Giant Burrowing Cockroach

Macropanesthia rhinoceros

What's in a name?

Macropanesthia means 'large wood-eating' and **rhinoceros** means 'nose-horned' and is possibly a reference to the accentuated 'scoop' on the male's carapace.

This insect is also known as the 'rhinoceros cockroach' or 'litter bug.'

The name of the order **Blattodea** is derived from the word **Blatta**, which is Latin for an insect which 'shuns the light.'

'One of my favourite Australian invertebrates.'

Classification

KINGDOM:	Animalia
PHYLUM:	Arthropoda
CLASS:	Insecta
ORDER:	Blattodea
FAMILY:	Blaberidae
GENUS:	*Macropanesthia*
SPECIES:	*rhinoceros*

Where is it found?

Cockroaches can be found throughout Australia, from the bush to our cities, however Giant Burrowing Cockroaches are a little more selective regarding where they live. They are found only in the tropical woodlands of far north Queensland. The humid understorey and blanket of leaves covering the forest floor is a paradise for these huge insects. They usually build their homes beneath the ground in eucalypt forests and their tunnels can be as long as 6m and as deep as 1m underground.

Amazing morphology and adaptations

These incredible arthropods are our environmental friend. They're native, don't lay eggs, and are the world's heaviest species of cockroach. They can grow up to the size of an adult human's hand.

Belonging to the phylum Arthropoda means that this powerful invertebrate has an exoskeleton and segmented legs. Giant Burrowing Cockroaches are insects and have three main body parts: the head, thorax, and abdomen; they also have six legs and a pair of antennae. These cockroaches are subterranean and spend most of their lives living beneath the ground. Their short, strong, spiky legs help them to dig tunnels, while the first pair of legs also has spikes similar in shape to the fingers on a human hand.

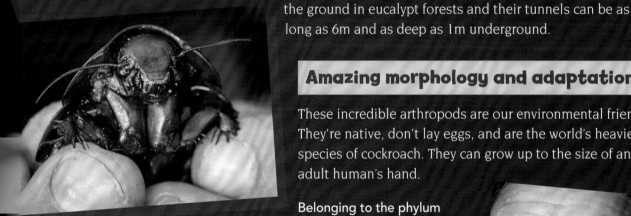

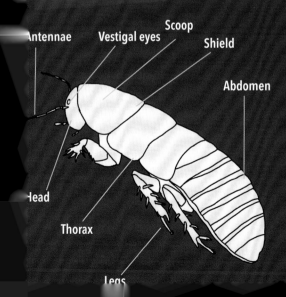

Antennae

Vestigal eyes

Scoop

Shield

Abdomen

Head

Thorax

Legs

Giant Burrowing Cockroaches collect all of their food from the ground. They have no wings and cannot fly.

Cockroaches have been around for 320 million years and their closest relatives are the termites. If the word cockroach gives you the shivers don't worry, you're not alone.

They don't need to shave their hairy legs – they use them to feel their way around.

There are more than 4,600 different species of cockroaches found throughout the world, and only four of them are considered pests.

The rest are just going about their jobs, keeping our natural world healthy.

Because of their size Giant Burrowing Cockroaches are a favourite prey item for various species of birds and lizards. To avoid being eaten they only come out at night when most animals have gone to sleep. If they are spotted, they rely on their hard exoskeleton that extends above their head to protect them from predators.

Unfortunately, cockroaches have a bit of an image problem, but most people don't seem to understand them.

They will also emit a loud hissing sound to scare animals away if they are harassed. They do this by squeezing air out of their abdomen.

They emerge at night-time to gather their food, which lucky for them is the abundant fallen dry gum leaves on the forest floor. They are such important animals in their ecosystem. They are known as **detritivores**, which means that they consume vegetation waste, and recycle the nutrients, releasing it back into the environment.

For such a tiny animal it really does have such a **HUGE** job to do. So many other plants and animals benefit from this amazing insect going about its business.

These giant insects have little use for their eyes in their dark subterranean world. Their eyes are vestigial, meaning that they are remnant, and don't see as such, only detecting lightness and darkness.

They employ long **antennae** – kind of like TV aerials – to feel their way around with.

The cockroach mouth has powerful mandibles for chewing decaying vegetative matter. Their thick abdomen is filled with fat reserves. This clever energy store helps them to survive when times are tough.

The large 'scoop' on their thorax, found near the top of their heads, can distinguish the males from the females. The females have little to no scoop while the males will have a much larger dent visible.

Giant Burrowing Cockroach is regarded as the world's heaviest cockroach species. They can live for more than ten years.

It looks like a mini skateboard ramp attached to their heads.

Life cycle

Giant Burrowing Cockroaches are what we call hemimetabolous.

Female with eggs

> It sounds like 'hemi-meta-ball-oss.'

This means that unlike some other insects, such as butterflies, they don't have a caterpillar or larval life stage. They begin life as an egg but their mother won't lay those eggs. Instead she will carry them inside her until they hatch then she will 'give birth' to up to 30 live young.

Nymphs

Adult female

Adult male

> **This is known as ovovivipary.**

Threats

Overcollection for the pet trade has had a negative impact on populations of Giant Burrowing Cockroaches in some areas.

Habitat destruction is continuing at an alarming rate across the entire range of this spectacular bug.

Introduced predators such as cats and foxes have been known to prey on this invertebrate.

After heavy rains, Giant Burrowing Cockroaches are flooded out of their subterranean burrows, seeking refuge on higher ground which is often busy highways and roads. Sadly, this cockroach falls victim to being driven over and killed by people's vehicles.

The young are called nymphs, and Giant Burrowing Cockroaches keep their nymphs inside a burrow up to a metre underground in order to protect them. The young nymphs will stay there while the parents bring them food, even breaking up the leaves into smaller parts for them. As they grow larger, the young become too big for their hard exoskeletons and will moult or shed their skin to reveal a new larger one underneath. Their new exoskeleton can take couple days to harden.

Giant Burrowing Cockroaches are **nocturnal**, which means that they hide and rest during the day and come out at night to look for food.

SCAN HERE
to watch a WILD clip

ikemic

Index

First published in 2021 by Reed New Holland Publishers Pty Ltd
Sydney • Auckland

Level 1, 178 Fox Valley Road, Wahroonga, NSW 2076, Australia
5/39 Woodside Avenue, Northcote, Auckland 0627, New Zealand
www.newhollandpublishers.com

A record of this book is held at the National Library of Australia.

ISBN 978 1 92554 670 5

Managing Director: Fiona Schultz
Publisher and Project Editor: Simon Papps
Designer: Andrew Davies
Production Director: Arlene Gippert
Printed in China

10 9 8 7 6 5 4 3 2

Keep up with New Holland Publishers:

NewHollandPublishers and ReedNewHolland

@newhollandpublishers